The Sounds of Silencing:

How Child Abuse Victims

Are Prevented

From

Speaking Out

Terri Austin, Ph.D., J.D.

© 2015

CONTENTS

PART III : Resources

Disclaimer

This book is a work of non-fiction. The author has interviewed and advocated on behalf of hundreds of abuse victims over the past four decades including survivors of domestic violence, child abuse, rape, bullying, stalking, and human trafficking.

The para-phrased accounts in this book have come from transcriptions of live interviews conducted for research purposes. In order to protect the abuse survivors' privacy, no actual names or locations will be used. Any resemblances to persons or legal cases can be presumed coincidental.

Relevant validation quotes are included after most of the Survivor's statements. Unless otherwise indicated these quotes are from Anonymous

authors.

Introduction

There are many forms of child abuse and interpersonal violence, including: emotional, verbal, sexual, physical, neglect, and forcing a child to witness violence and abuse done to others. The common denominator of all types of abuse is Silence.

Survivors of child abuse comprise an endless list of people who experienced the types of abuse listed above, as well as those who had parent(s) with Narcissistic or Antisocial Personality Disorders since these disorders have inherent a lack of empathy, disregard for others' feelings, and self-serving manipulation of people.

Silencing methods comprise a list ranging from subtle non-verbal facial expressions to the ultimate form of silencing----- outright murder, the imposition of "dead silencing"------ by the abuser. There are statements such as, "Be quiet," "Don't tell," "Don't cry," Shut up about it;" threats such as, "I'll hurt you if you tell," "Something bad will happen to your family," "I'll kill your dog;" tactics like denial, minimizing, de-humanizing, shaming, discrediting, attacking victims' self-esteem, sabotaging victims' attempts at healing, slandering, defaming, and blaming the victims. Some children are victimized before they can even speak to object to or disclose abusive behaviors. Others are prevented from saying "no" by parents who have taught them to be overly compliant. Additionally, there are agencies that refuse to investigate, report, or take action against predators----often within their own ranks---- thus enabling and becoming accessories to the abuser's crimes.

As for victim homicide, typically a child goes missing and after a few days is still not found. A late friend of mine----co-educator and founder of a Search and Rescue Dog agency----has said that if a missing child isn't located within the first 48 hours, chances are (s)he has already been killed. Offenders used to bribe kids with candy or dollar bills; nowadays, it's $50 - $100 bills----and "Come and see the puppies in my van....."

Children have been abducted from school, home, playgrounds, movie theaters and other places in broad daylight by not only the stereotypical perverted stranger----but by friends, relatives, and trusted professionals, who sexually abused and subsequently killed them. Sex offenders have also included teenagers. Just last week, a breaking news story featured the sexual homicide of a local 9-year-old girl by a teenager who resided in the same apartment complex.

By the time most survivors of abuse are able to talk about their experiences, it will usually be after years of psychotherapy; sometimes years of

having to take medication for symptoms of Post-
Traumatic

Stress Disorder. Quite often those years turn into

decades.......and this is where the Statute of

Limitations comes into play, protecting the

abusers, as opposed to helping survivors. In many

civil settlements the conditions might include

confidentiality orders which forbid survivors to

discuss their experiences or publicly identify their

abusers. The Statute of Limitations on child abuse

crimes, as well as gag orders and Civil

Compromise Confidentiality Conditions related to

these incidents, are barriers to healing and need to

be abolished nationwide for the benefit of the

survivors and the protection of other potential victims.

I would like to make reference to the text of the first verse of the song *The Sound of Silence* (Simon and Garfunkel). The lyrics to the song can be found on the recording artists' publisher's website (MCA Publishing www.mcapublishing.com .) Although this song was not written about child abuse, it pertains to Oppression; aka----silencing.

My "vision" is that someday the Statute of Limitations for child abuse crimes, along with anything else pertaining to these offenses, which prevent and/or forbid victims and survivors from speaking out, will be abolished; this vision "still remains within the sound of silence"……in that it

has yet to happen.

PART I : RELEVANT TOPICS

Narcissistic Personality Disorder

In the American Psychiatric Association's Diagnostic and Statistical Manual of Mental Disorders, Fifth Edition (DSM-V), Narcissistic Personality Disorder (hereinafter NPD) is defined as a pervasive pattern of grandiosity (in fantasy or behavior), a constant need for admiration, and a lack of empathy, beginning by early adulthood and present in a variety of contexts, including:

• A grandiose sense of self-importance;

• A preoccupation with fantasies of unlimited success, power,

brilliance, beauty, or ideal love;

• A belief that he or she is special and unique

and can only be understood by, or should

associate with, other special or high- status people

or institutions;

  • A need for excessive admiration;

  • A sense of entitlement;

  • Interpersonally exploitive behavior;

  • A lack of empathy;

  • Envy of others or a belief that others are

envious of him or her;

  • A demonstration of arrogant and haughty

behaviors or attitudes;

In addition, NPD is characterized by the

presence of both grandiosity and attention seeking.

Parental Narcissistic Emotional Abuse

This invariably goes hand-in-hand with Narcissistic Personality Disorder and is a more severe level of abuse simply because of the inherent incurable personality disorder factor, the behaviors of which manifest on a daily basis as a combination of deliberate and unconscious motivations.

Children narcissistic parent(s) (or caregivers)

fear that if they discuss their parent's behavior to anyone outside of the family, no one will listen or believe them. Unfortunately, in many cases this is true, since the NPD parent can present a good public image. Additionally, the child is terrified about consequences they will incur if their complaint to third parties gets back to his or her parent(s).

There are six common types of emotional abuse (Tuthill, O. 1998): Rejecting, Neglect and Ignoring, Terrorizing, Isolating, Corrupting, and Exploiting. Emotionally abusive behaviors include bullying, humiliating, constant criticism, demeaning, manipulating, scapegoating, name-calling, innuendos, sarcastic put-downs, and overcontrolling.

I would like to add the following emotionally abusive behaviors to those manifested by Narcissistic Personality Disordered parents: Sabotage and Taking-Away; and Identity Theft.

Sabotage and Taking-Away include parent(s) interference with a child's progress toward something that the child likes and wants. This happens when parents feel threatened by the child's desires and goals because the insecure parent is not the center of the child's attention. This could be about a hobby, academics, friendships, an activity, a goal, or a possession. For example----

Narcissistic Mother might feel jealous of her 4-year-old daughter spending a lot of time playing with a favorite doll. She might restrict the time the little girl is allowed to play with the doll (for no reason, or for a fictitious reason); she might verbally demean the child for playing with the doll so much; at some point will hide the doll from the child, or throw it away and pretend not to know what happened to it. An interviewee of mine described this scenario, recalling it from when she was a child; however, after her Narcissistic Mother disposed of the doll she accused my client of being "irresponsible" and "not knowing how to take care of (her) toys" and told her not to talk about it ever again-----basically blaming the victim, then silencing her.

Another survivor of emotional abuse by Narcissistic Parents described how his abuse manifested as a failure, on the parents part, to encourage him to explore and possibly pursue a career as a professional musician. They never took him to----nor allowed him to go to----performances by his favorite professional recording artist. They didn't allow him to play in public weekend "gigs" with his high school band members. His parents seemed to frequently find ways to sabotage his attendance at extra-curricular band practices. He described the situation as one of learned-helplessness wherein eventually he stopped pursuing his goal.

Some Narcissistic parents fear a child's eventual separation and independence because the parent fears a loss of control over the child. Another interviewee described how his mother refused to allow him to get a weekend job when he was in high school. She did not want him to become capable of earning his own money----- but then she accused him of being "immature" and a "freeloader" when he asked for allowance. He recalled being embarrassed because most of his friends had weekend jobs, or worked after school, whereas he did not. When his school counselor discussed the situation with my client's mother, she decided that he could have a "job"-----it was a volunteer, non-paid part-time position stocking shelves in a thrift store at which one of her friends was the manager.

Identity Theft in the emotional abuse sense is just like its criminal counterpart. This happens when a parent "steals" the child's identity by imitating or competing with the child. For example----a mother who imitates her teenaged daughter's clothing style, hairstyle, and//or interests and hobbies. The parent(s) goal----whether conscious or unconscious----is to prevent the child from becoming a separate individual. Consider the teenager who plays on the school tennis team whose mother suddenly becomes "interested" in tennis to the point of taking private lessons (she can afford lessons for herself but not for her teenager!) and states her intention of becoming a champion at Wimbleton tournaments. Are we surprised when her teenager eventually quits the school tennis team? A very common survival strategy for teenagers who are in this Identity Theft situation is to identify with something which the parent(s) totally despises and wouldn't make the effort to "steal."

Needless to say, emotional abuse by Narcissistic

Personality Disorder Parents is associated with

significant damage to children who experience it.

Stockholm Syndrome

Stockholm Syndrome is considered to be the ultimate survival strategy for victims of abuse. The term originated from an incident in Stockholm, Sweden, in 1973 wherein hostages were confined to a bank's vault for a period of six days in what is known as the Norrmalmstorg Robbery. The captors strapped dynamite to the hostages and set up snare traps so that, in the event of any law enforcement rescue attempts, the hostages would be killed. Throughout the ordeal the hostages psychologically bonded with their captors to the point of becoming friends with them and manifesting resistance to being rescued.

When the captors were eventually arrested, the hostages set up a fund to assist with legal fees, and supported these people throughout the court process. Later, one of the hostages married one of the captors.

This syndrome is a type of paradoxical, unconscious psychological and emotional bonding which can occur between victims and abusers in situations where there is an imbalance of power. The victim who perceives that (s)he cannot escape from the situation minimizes the dangerousness of it. (S)he focuses on the "positive" qualities and small kindnesses of the abuser to the point of believing that the abuser loves him or her, and will go as far as attempting to protect the abuser from criminal prosecution. Victims who develop Stockholm Syndrome have an extremely difficult time psychologically separating from the abuser. It is not uncommon for them to continue to protect the abuser for many years, even despite physical separation.

Child abuse victims, hostages, prisoners of war, and cult members learn to develop cognitive and behavioral survival strategies so as to minimize pain and tolerate their abuse situation over which they perceive they have no control or means of escape. Survival strategies have included denial, silence, dissociation, and increased tolerance of the situation to the point of

believing that it is normal without realizing that

damage is actually occurring.

<u>Psychopathy</u>

The term psychopathy, by itself, is not a diagnosis. It refers to aspects of a personality disorder that includes a cluster of interpersonal, affective, lifestyle, and antisocial traits and behaviors. Psychopathy involves deception; manipulation; irresponsibility; impulsivity; stimulation seeking; poor behavioral controls; shallow affect; lack of empathy, guilt, or remorse; sexual promiscuity; and callous disregard for the rights of others.

To understand psychopathy, it is necessary to know some basic principles about personality. Individuals' personalities represent who they are;

they result from genetics and upbringing and reflect how people interact with others and cope with problems, both real and imagined. Individuals' personalities develop and evolve until approximately their late 20s, after which they are well-ingrained, for the most part unable to be altered.

Psychopathy traits begin to manifest in early childhood and ultimately define adult psychopathy. The lifelong expression of this disorder is a product of complex interactions between biological and temperamental predispositions and social forces---- e.g., nature and nurture.

Many psychopaths exhibit a profound lack of

remorse for their aggressive actions, both violent and nonviolent, along with a lack of empathy for their victims. This enables them to act in a cold-blooded manner, using those around them as pawns to achieve goals and satisfy needs and desires, whether sexual, financial, physical, or emotional. Most psychopaths are grandiose, selfish sensation seekers who lack a conscience. They do not accept responsibility for their actions, instead shifting the blame to someone or something else.

In DSM-V, psychopathy is one of five dimensions for describing a personality disorder, officially acknowledged by American psychiatry after approximately fifty years of research.

Antisocial Personality Disorder

According to the DSM-V, there are four main diagnostic criterion, for this disorder.

A. <u>Disregard for and violation of others rights since age 15, as indicated by one of the seven sub features</u>:

1. Failure to obey laws and norms by engaging in behavior which results in criminal arrest, or would warrant arrest by law enforcement;

2. Lying, deception, and manipulation, for profit tor self-amusement;

3. Impulsive behavior;

4. Irritability and aggression, manifested as

frequently assaulting others, or engaging in fighting;

    5. Blatant disregard for safety of self and others;

    6. A pattern of irresponsibility;

    7. Lack of remorse for actions;

The other diagnostic Criterion are:

    B. <u>The person is at least age 18</u>;

    C. <u>Conduct disorder was present before age 15</u>;

    D. <u>And the antisocial behavior does not occur in the context of</u>

        <u>schizophrenia or bipolar disorder.</u>

    The DSM-V notes that Antisocial Personality

Disorder cannot be diagnosed before age 18. If an

adolescent displays antisocial features prior to age

18, if diagnostic criteria are met, the appropriate

diagnosis would be Conduct Disorder.

Most prison inmates meet the criteria for a

diagnosis of Antisocial Personality Disorder.

Post-Traumatic Stress Disorder

In 2013, the American Psychiatric Association revised the PTSD diagnostic criteria in the fifth edition of its Diagnostic and Statistical Manual of Mental Disorders (DSM-V). The diagnostic criteria specified below are specific to adults, adolescents, and children older than six years. There is a separate subtype for children under the age of six.

Criterion A: stressor

The person was exposed to: death, threatened death, actual or threatened serious injury, or actual or threatened sexual violence, as follows:

1. Direct exposure.

2. Witnessing, in person.

3. Indirectly, by learning that a close relative or close friend was exposed to trauma. If the event involved actual or threatened death, it must have been violent or accidental.

4. Repeated or extreme indirect exposure to aversive details of the event(s), usually in the course of professional duties (e.g., first responders, collecting body parts; professionals repeatedly exposed to details of child abuse). This does not include indirect non-professional exposure through electronic media, television, movies, or pictures.

Criterion B: intrusion symptoms

The traumatic event is persistently re-experienced in the following way(s):

1. Recurrent, involuntary, and intrusive memories. Note: Children older than six may express this symptom in repetitive play.

2. Traumatic nightmares. Note: Children may have frightening dreams without content related to the trauma(s).

3. Dissociative reactions (e.g., flashbacks)

which may occur on a

continuum from brief episodes to complete

loss of consciousness.

4. Intense or prolonged distress after

exposure to traumatic reminders.

5. Marked physiologic reactivity after

exposure to trauma-related stimuli.

Criterion C: avoidance

Persistent effortful avoidance of distressing

trauma-related stimuli after the event:

1. Trauma-related thoughts or feelings.

2. Trauma-related external reminders (e.g.,

people, places, conversations, activities, objects,

or situations).

Criterion D: negative alterations in cognitions and mood

Negative alterations in cognitions and mood that began or worsened after the traumatic event:

1. Inability to recall key features of the traumatic event (usually dissociative amnesia; not due to head injury, alcohol, or drugs).

2. Persistent (and often distorted) negative beliefs and expectations about oneself or the world (e.g., "I am bad,"

"The world is completely dangerous").

3. Persistent distorted blame of self or others for causing the traumatic event or for resulting consequences.

4. Persistent negative trauma-related emotions (e.g., fear, horror, anger, guilt, or shame).

5. Markedly diminished interest in (pre-traumatic) significant activities.

6. Feeling alienated from others (e.g., detachment or estrangement).

7. Constricted affect: persistent inability to experience positive emotions.

Criterion E: alterations in arousal and reactivity

Trauma-related alterations in arousal and reactivity that began or worsened after the traumatic event:

1. Irritable or aggressive behavior

2. Self-destructive or reckless behavior

3. Hypervigilance

4. Exaggerated startle response

5. Problems in concentration

6. Sleep disturbance

Criterion F: duration

Persistence of symptoms for more than one month.

Criterion G: functional significance

Significant symptom-related distress or functional impairment (e.g., social, occupational).

Criterion H: exclusion

Disturbance is not due to medication, substance use, or other illness.

Full diagnosis is not met until at least six months after the trauma(s), although onset of symptoms may occur immediately.

Statute of Limitations

A type of federal or state law that restricts the time within which legal proceedings may be brought. The statute of limitations is a defense that is ordinarily asserted by the defendant in a civil or criminal proceeding to defeat an action brought against him after the appropriate time has elapsed. Therefore, the defendant must plead the defense before the court upon answering the plaintiff's complaint. If the defendant does not do so, he is regarded as having waived the defense and will not be permitted to use it in any subsequent proceedings.

To find the Statute of Limitations for your

State, go to this link: www.SOLreform.com .

Criminal Actions

A majority of states have a statute of limitations for all crimes except murder. Once the statute has expired, the court lacks jurisdiction to try or punish a defendant.

Criminal statutes of limitations apply to different crimes on the basis of their general classification as either felonies or misdemeanors.

Generally, the time limit starts to run on the date the offense was committed, not from the time the crime was discovered or the accused was identified.

Civil Actions

In determining which statute of limitations will control in a civil action, the type of Cause of Action that the claim will be pursued under is critical. Different deadlines are established depending on whether the cause of action involves a contract, personal injury, libel, fraud, or other claim. (www.law.cornell.edu ; www.law.com)

Civil Compromise Conditions

This is a type of settlement agreement wherein the parties to a lawsuit agree to resolve the issues amicably, usually with the Plaintiff and/or insurance company agreeing to dismiss the

44

case, and pay the Plaintiff a certain amount of money in exchange for releasing the Defendant from liability. Cases may be settled at any time prior to or during litigation or trial, and prior to or after an appeal.

In cases such as child abuse where the Plaintiffs frequently don't come forward with the details of the offense for years after the Statute of Limitations has run, attorneys are often inclined to settle these cases. Unfortunately for the Plaintiffs, one of the conditions of settlement may include Confidentiality so as to protect the Defendant's reputation and not disclose his/her identity. Confidentiality Conditions also usually entail nondisclosure of the monetary amount of settlement. A further disadvantage to Plaintiffs is a Liquidated Damages clause in a settlement which basically states that if the Defendant can prove that the Plaintiff breached the Confidentiality agreement, the Plaintiff will owe the Defendant monetary damages to be determined by the court, <u>whether or not the Defendant can prove damage to his/her reputation or any other injury.</u>

Confidentiality Conditions and Liquidated Damages clauses usually tend to apply mutually to the Plaintiffs and Defendants; the idea is that both parties will be protected. In my opinion----and likewise that of many abuse survivors----these

Conditions of settlements do more harm than good for the Plaintiffs, because the Plaintiffs are in effect paid to remain silent.

Gag Order

A court order prohibiting the attorneys and the parties to a lawsuit or criminal prosecution from talking to the media or the public about the case. The supposed intent is to prevent prejudice due to pre-trial publicity which would influence potential jurors. Based on the "freedom of the press" provision of the First Amendment, the court cannot constitutionally restrict the media from printing or broadcasting information about the case, so the only way is to put a gag on the participants under the court's control.

(www.law.cornell.edu ; www.law.com)

48

Erin's Law

Erin Merryn, a survivor of childhood rape and incest, has advocated since 2009 to get states to adopt legislation which would require schools to teach age-appropriate curriculum on child sex abuse prevention.

As of this date, many states have implemented versions of the legislation, known as Erin's Law. A version of Erin's Law was passed in California last spring, whereby educators will receive training related to child abuse prevention, and by 2018 students in grades Pre-K-12 will begin receiving curricula about personal body safety. According to Merryn, this curriculum is not sex

49

education. Children will be taught that it is inappropriate to let people touch the areas covered by their swimsuits and to distinguish between safe and unsafe touches. Children will also be taught the importance of reporting abuse.

The partial text of Erin's Law in California reads as follows:

(This law) *Requires the state board, based upon recommendations by the superintendent of Public Instruction, to consider including age-appropriate content for kindergarten and grades 1 to 12, inclusive, in sexual abuse and sexual assault awareness and prevention in the next*

revision of the health content standards. Requires

the state board, based upon recommendations by

the commission, to consider including information

in sexual abuse and sexual assault awareness and

prevention in the Health Framework for California

Public Schools when next revised. Authorizes

school districts, county offices of education, and

charter schools to provide age-appropriate

instruction, pursuant to the content standards

adopted by the state board, for kindergarten and

grades 1 to 12, inclusive, as applicable, in sexual

abuse and sexual assault awareness and

prevention. Provides a procedure for excusing a

pupil from that instruction (California Assembly Bill 2016, Chapter 809.)

This wonderful law will help empower children who are victims of abuse to speak up.

PART II : SURVIVORS' STORIES

Freedom of Speech?
Male, age 34

"Congress shall make no law respecting an establishment of religion, or prohibiting the free exercise thereof; or abridging the freedom of speech, or of the press; or the right of the people peaceably to assemble, and to petition the Government for a redress of grievances."

(U.S. Constitution - Amendment 1
Proposed 9/25/1789
Ratified 12/15/1791)

The United States Constitution states that these are

guaranteed rights. If this is the case, then

why are child abuse victims' freedom of

speech rights taken away by gag-orders?

All it does is prevent closure. Victims can't

own their story

because they have to keep on protecting the

abusers by keeping

secrets. It's the <u>criminal</u> justice system----not

the victims'

justice system.

It isn't fair.

"The very first part in healing is shattering the silence."
(Erin Merryn, 2014 / Erin's Law)

"Everyone has the right to tell the truth about her own life."
(Ellen Bass / The Courage to Heal)

"He who accepts evil without protesting against it is really cooperating with it."
(Martin Luther King)

Don't Tell Anybody
Male, age 19

"Don't tell anybody about........."

Things that happen at home;

What the P.E. teacher does with a couple of

 boys after school,

when everyone else has gone home;

The wild parties and sex movies the priest

shows on campouts

 that only certain kids get invited to;

"Because if you tell...."

You'll get beat up;

Nobody's gonna believe you;

Things will get worse;

You could get killed;

The priest will move to a different church;

The P.E. teacher will get fired;

"…….and it'll be all YOUR fault."

"Never be silent just because someone else wants you to be."

"I will not stay silent so that you can stay comfortable."

Tired of Bad News
Female, age 18

You know how my mother treats me when

she's done crack----

throws dishes at me, calls me names,

always putting me down,

accuses me of doing things I didn't do,

treats me like shit.

I tried to tell my shrink about this. Want to

know

what he said?

He said, "I'm tired of hearing bad news. Come

back

and see me when

you have some good news."

Hey----I never went back. What the hell kind of

doctor only sees "healthy" patients???

I found out later on that shrinks are <u>mandated</u>

 reporters;

They have a legal duty to report

suspected

child abuse.

He never reported my mother.

*"The way people treat you is a statement
about who they are. It is
not about you."*

Actions Speak
Male, age 17

My parents are always fighting.

Dad gets violent, starts yelling at mom and us

 kids.

Sometimes he hits mom. One time he tried to

run over me with his car because

I was in his way,

riding my scateboard in the driveway.

I keep hoping things will change for the better-

---maybe he'll

stop drinking, move out, or something.

I'm not supposed to talk about this stuff.

Dad says he'll kick my ass if I tell anybody,

because

It will ruin his reputation and he could get

kicked off

the School Board.

My best friend knows about all this;

he's been over when

they were fighting.

I just keep my mouth shut, cover up for them

whenever I need to.

But it comes out anyway----all the anger,

resentment, confusion, pain, sadness,

frustration-----when

I get into trouble at school.

Everyone says I'm the one with the problem.

I'm the one who needs to see a counselor.

The principal tells me my parents will be

very disappointed in me.

"Every word, facial expression, gesture, or action on the partof a parent gives the child some message about self-worth. It is sad that so many parents don't realize what messages they are sending."
(Maya Angelou)

"Unexpressed emotions will never die. They are buried alive and will come forth later in uglier ways."
(Sigmund Freud)

Teddy Bears
Female, age 29

I used to cry in bed some nights,

praying to God that

someone would love me for real.

I was 10 years old.

Confused about why my parents

would tell me they love me,

but then act so mean to me.

I'd whisper this stuff privately

 to my teddy bears.

Teddy bears never criticize;

they can be trusted with

secrets nobody else would want

 to know about.

My teddy bears loved me.

Thank God for teddy bears!

"Teddy, I've been bad again. My mom told me so; I'm not quite sure what I did wrong, but I thought that you might know. When I woke up this morning, I knew that she was mad; because she was crying awfully hard, and yelling at my dad. I tried my best to be real good and do just what she said. I cleaned my room all by myself; and I even made my bed. But I spilled milk on my good shirt when she yelled at me to hurry; and I guess she didn't hear me when I told her I was sorry, because she hit me awfully hard, and called me funny names, and told me I was really bad and I should be ashamed. When I said 'I love you, mom' I guess she didn't really understand, because she yelled at me to shut my mouth or I'd get smacked again. So I came up here to talk to you. Please tell me what to do, because I really love my mom, and I know she loves me, too. I don't think my mom means to hit me quite so hard; I guess sometimes grown-ups forget how big they really are. So, Teddy, I wish you were real and you weren't just a bear. Then you could help me find a way to tell moms everywhere. So please try hard to understand how sad it makes me feel. The outside pain soon goes away, but the inside never heals. And if we could make them listen, maybe then they'd understand, so other kids just like me wouldn't have to hurt again. But for now, I guess I'll hold you tight and pretend the pain's not there. I know you'd never hurt me......I love you; so goodnight, Teddy Bear."

Little Man of the House
Male, age 25

I became the new Man of the House since

mom and dad divorced.

My job was to lift heavy stuff, take the

 garbage out to the curb,

wash mom's car, clean the garage.

I also had to comfort mom when she was

 upset; she complained

about dad a lot, told me all kinds of stuff

that wasn't really any of

my business.

Sometimes there'd be advantages------

like I'd get

more privileges

than my sisters and younger brother.

But most of the time I didn't like being the new

Man of the House.

I was only 9 years old.

"It has been said that time heals all wounds. I do not agree. The wounds remain; in time the mind, protecting its sanity, covers them with scar tissue and the pain lessens. But it is never gone."

(Rose Kennedy)

Obligation
Female, age 37

My school counselor was 27; I was 13.

I thought he was SO cool! He was someone

I could trust----

he never busted me

for smoking pot at school.

 I could tell him just about anything

and he wouldn't turn me in.

He said anytime I wanted to "legitimately" cut

classes all I had to

do was ask the teacher for a hall pass to his

office; he'd write me

clearances for my absences from class.

I'd hang around at his office a lot.

One day he came on to me; we had sex.

I thought this was love.

I kept our secret for years......so that <u>he</u>

wouldn't get busted.

I felt I owed it to him.

"Stockholm Syndrome does not equal true love."

"Over time, you'll start to notice that some people just aren't worth it anymore."

"The problem is that I care way too much about people who don't give a shit about me."

Stolen Childhood
Female, age 41

My parents' needs always came first,

when I was a kid.

I couldn't just be a "regular" third grader

like my friends and classmates.

It was like I had to take care of mom and dad.

They discussed their personal problems

with me; the budget; work issues.

I remember walking downtown to hand-deliver

some of their monthly bill payments-----they

said it saved them gas and postage stamps

when I did this.

But I wasn't allowed to walk a few blocks

to go to my friend's birthday parties.

My parents were able to save on gas

and postage.

I'm the one who was ripped off;

my childhood

was stolen, and I never got

reimbursement.

"The worst people in the world are the ones who steal childhood from children."

"It's because of you that I spent so many years feeling worthless. You stole those years from me."

Protection
Female Inmate, age 36

I didn't get allowance. Us kids weren't allowed

to have jobs, either.

My parents bought me stuff but didn't like

for me to have my own money. Whenever

I got any money, I hid it.

As a teenager I found out that sex and drugs

were worth a lot of money.

An older guy in his thirties

whom I met at a beach

party taught me how to make money this way.

He got me a job working for him,

selling dope and getting

paid for sex at parties.

I had to give him most of what I got paid, but

He also paid me and bought me nice clothes.

He said I could get arrested or even killed

 if I told any of my friends that I

worked for him;

he said his friends who looked out for him

would kill me.

I learned that I could make more money in

 a week than the teachers at my school

 made in a month.

And sure as hell lots more than the shrink

who was trying to talk me into going to

college to get an education and a good

job. What the fuck do I need a job

and college for?

"Human Trafficking is the fastest growing criminal industry in the world, second to the drug trade."

"There is a hell. Believe me, I've seen it."

Depression
Female, age 46

I've been depressed ever since

I was a little kid,

before and after going to foster care.

My parents

drank and did drugs. Dad was in and

out of prison

for gang stuff. Mom and dad were always

yelling at and hitting us kids for any little

thing that pissed them off.

We even got hit for no reason.

Couldn't do anything right, nothing

ever pleased them unless it was something

that made them look

good. Teachers told my parents

that something was wrong,

that maybe I was depressed

when I overdosed on aspirin at school.

But who wants to be the "parents of a

depressed kid"??

They must've thought if they ignored

the depression

it would go away on its own.

It didn't.

I got treatment when I turned 21, without the

parents' knowledge. I've been taking

anti-depressants

since then.

There was an old experiment done with dogs.

They got electric shocks whether

they moved to the left or

right side of their cage. Damned if they

did or didn't.

That's what depression feels like.

"A tear is made of 1% water......and 99% feelings."

"To anyone who has ever made me feel like my best wasn't good enough: Fuck you!"

"The proverbial double-bind is a form of control without open coercion.. It is using a manipulation tactic without looking like you are manipulating. It's being put in a damned if we do, damned if we don't situation; and damned if you say anything about it."

"Grab a plate and throw it on the ground. If it broke, apologize to it. Did it go back to the way it was? Now do you understand?"

"Freedom's just another word for nothing left to lose."

(Janis Joplin)

"Depression doesn't mean you are weak. It means you've been strong for too long."

The Bad Word
Female, age 24

Not overseas, but right here in town.

Accomplices in crime: a cop and the

Assistant Chief of Police.

They threw wild parties at each others'

houses----only the "good old boys"

were invited.

Showed porno films borrowed from

the police evidence locker;

sold dope in a back

bathroom; hired teenage girls

for sexual services.......girls

who had reputations for minor crimes:

curfew violations, ditching school,

fighting, shoplifting,

running away from home,

fighting; stuff like that.

The cops' cover-up was pre-meditated

in case any of us girls

decided to report them

so nobody would believe us : "These girls

make false police reports"

is what they planned on saying.

They also threatened to have us killed

if we ever told-----

said they had connections to contract killers;

all they had to do was put

The Bad Word out on us and

 we'd be dead in 24-hours.

They had NO right to make us remain silent

 like that;

setting us up

so as not to be able to get help when we

 needed it!

"Don't ever be afraid to call the police

 if you need us. That's

what we're here for," they said.

Perhaps they expected us to take a joke........

"If you blame the victim, you have become an accomplice."

"Abusive people have unwritten rules. One big unwritten rule is the rule of silence. I know this silence well; it was a big part of my life for a very long time. The victim knows the rules of silence and generally complies with them for fear of more abuse, or embarrassment by the abuser, which is also abuse. The silencing plan included spinning the truth to the point of making it seem like everything is the victim's fault. This fear keeps the victim quiet. It's highly effective."

(Tricia Johnson)

"You have the right to remain silent. Anything you say will be misquoted and used against you."

"Mean people don't bother me. It's the mean people who disguise themselves as nice people who bother me a lot."

Everyone Believes A Priest
Male, age 31

Fr. Bob molests young altar boys.

Tells them God will

hate them and send them to hell

if they rat him out.

Everyone thinks Fr. Bob is the greatest.

I wanted to tell on him, but didn't think

 anybody

would believe me.

My day to tell on him came 26 years later,

 after other young men came forward.

Fr. Bob denied everything, of course.

The Diocese settled the cases out of court.

Small change awards

for the victims;

the Statute of Limitations

had passed a long time ago.

Fr. Bob got transferred to another church in

another part of the state. He still molests

 boys;

he's not gonna change.

Everybody believes a priest........and

 somebody needs

to speak up for all these boys.

"Child molesters are not cured. They just get better at hiding it. Don't be fooled."

"The greater the power, the more dangerous the abuse."

(Edmund Burke)

"The world is a dangerous place to live; not because of the people who are evil, but because of the people who don't do anything about it.

(A. Einstein)

"Since the primary motive of the evil is disguise, one of the places evil people are not likely to be found is within the church. What better way to conceal one's evil from oneself as well as from others than to be a deacon some other highly visible form of Christian within our culture."

(Dr. M. Scott Peck)

"If you remain neutral in situations of injustice, you have chosen the side of the oppressor."

(Desmond Tutu)

Self-Blame
Female, age 43

Narcissistic parents <u>cannot</u>:

Empathize; love; be honest;

focus on anything other

than themselves; admit that

they have problems.

I used to wonder what was wrong with ME-----

I wanted

to fix myself so I'd be good enough

for them.

It took me 22 years of counseling

to accept the fact

that I was ok.....to learn that NOTHING

 would ever be good enough

 for them.

It was <u>they</u>

 who couldn't be

fixed. Not ever.

Zebras don't change their stripes.

I wish I knew way back then

what I know now.

Maybe I can help others heal;

 young adults

with the same kind of parents that I had. So

that they won't have

to spend their whole lifetime

feeling bad

about themselves.

It's a life's worth of time

that nobody can ever

give back to you when

it's taken away

since the very beginning,

when you are born.

"Some of the most poisonous people come disguised as friends and family."

*"Be careful how you speak to your children.
One day it will become their inner voice."*

*"We can't help everyone, but everyone can
help someone."*

*"Afraid of monsters under my bed? Hell no----I
was raised by monsters."*

*"I may be the black sheep of the family, but
some of the white sheep aren't as white as they try
to appear."*

*"To come to terms with evil in one's parentage
is perhaps the most difficult and painful
psychological task a human being can be called
upon to face. Most fail and so remain its victims.
Those who fully succeed in developing the
necessary searing vision are those who
are able to name it."*

(Dr. M. Scott Peck)

Keeping Quiet
Male, age 32

He bought me cigarettes and beer;

gave me money to spend.

He gave me his private cell

phone number; I hung out at his place on

weekends and after school-----

if anybody asked, we'd

say he was helping me with homework.

We played computer games

and drank beer.

Sometimes he took a bunch

of us boys to ball games.

He told me I was

his favorite student.

He trusted me with more

stuff and gave me more privileges

than other kids.

He bought me expensive gifts.

He told me personal things about

other students.

 He smoked weed with me. I was his

teacher's aide, my junior year in high school.

He knew I didn't have a dad at home;

dad was doing

 time for armed robbery. I needed

 a father figure.

One day we started looking at

 porno magazines at his house….

One thing led to another.

"Don't tell anybody" went without saying.

 I needed him, so I kept quiet about

everything.

"Sometimes the person you'd take a bullet for ends up being the one shooting the gun."

"Our lives begin to end the day we become silent about things that matter."

"The trauma bond means that the victim may also wish to receive comfort from the very person who abused them, even though at some point the victim may disclose the abuse."

"Children don't lie about being sexually abused. They are made to lie in order to keep it a secret."

Set-Up
Female, age 29

Fr. Fred opened a youth center

for teenage boys.

People thought he might be gay;

but he said he wasn't.

He and I began dating after I turned 18;

he told me that he loved me

and was planning to quit his job as a priest.

People saw us together in theaters, fancy

restaurants, parties, and other events.

All "public appearances" for his benefit,

I later discovered; all a big set-up:

"He's with her all the time, so he must

not be gay, after all," is what he

wanted people to think.

Suddenly, without warning, he got moved to

a church in another town.

"But you said you were quitting……"

Confusion.

He never told me he was planning to leave

town. Told me to keep in touch.

Then he accused me of "stalking"-----

compiled false

evidence for the District Attorney;

crazy woman stalker.

Several years later, Fr. Fred's name came up;

a guy said he was

sexually abused

 by Fr. Fred as a teenager

at Fr. Fred's youth center, years ago.

Big lawsuit followed.

Out of court settlement.

So much for public appearances.

"When someone shows you who they are,
believe them the first time."

(Maya Angelou)

"I didn't deserve any of that shit."

"I am not to blame."

"Abusers control, manipulate, and make you feel like you are the one with the problem. Stand up, speak out and take back your life. You are not to blame."

<u>Repetitive Patterns</u>
Female, age 44

My ex-husband has Narcissistic Personality

Disorder. Just like my NPD mother.

All of the behavioral symptoms were

there, but I was in denial......because he was

not my mother.

I was blind to it all......unconsciously repeating

the pattern of my family dynamics.

I didn't know any better back then; but

I've definitely learned.

Maybe I can help other women learn.

"We all have the right to feel safe."

"A bird doesn't sing because it has an answer. It sings because it has a song."

(Maya Angelou)

"Narcissists don't walk; they slither.
Narcissists don't feel; they compute.
Narcissists don't like; they obsess.
Narcissists don't create; they plagiarize.
Narcissists don't listen; they hear.
Narcissists don't support; they manipulate.
Narcissists don't take pride; they take credit.
Narcissists don't teach; they misinform.
Narcissists don't love; they destroy.
Narcissists don't empathize; they compete."

Shut Up
Male Inmate, age 18

"Don't get angry," "Shut up! Don't

yell at your father----it's

disrespectful."

My father yells at me all the time;

cusses me out;

hits me when he's mad enough-----

calls it "discipline".

Isn't THAT disrespectful?

"Watch your tone of voice----don't argue!"

"That look on your face is hostile----quit

frowning."

So where does all of my suppressed anger

end up?

It comes out at school.

I don't go to class, I get in fights,

I destroy school

property, break windows, slash the

 principal's tires.

Most of the time I didn't get caught.

Sometimes my parents ask me, "How

 was school today?"

And I say, "It was ok."

"It takes 1000 'atta boy's to erase one 'you're an idiot' ."

"Abuse is about control. When done to children it can be disguised as Authority; but no matter what words are used to describe it, it is a black hole, a living hell, that a child is trapped in."

"When a child hits a child, we call it aggression. When a child hits an adult, we call it hostility. When an adult hits an adult, we call it assault and battery. When an adult hits a child, we call it discipline."

"Respect your kids. Too many adults demand respect from kids without showing any respect in return. Doesn't work that way."

(Lyle Perry)

People Don't Need to Know
Female Inmate, age 29

I was sexually involved with

older men since I was a little kid.

I never considered it abuse-----

they were mom's friends;

 they were nice to me, bought me toys,

said nice things to me. They gave my mom

a lot of money.

They weren't mean like my father

and step-father were, and they didn't

beat me like my father

and step-father did;

now THAT was abuse!

I couldn't tell ANYBODY about

these guys; mom said people

didn't need

to know about them.

She said they could

get in trouble because

 I was still a kid.

When I got into middle school,

the term "child abuse"

was floating around----but I still didn't

understand it.

There's no way that term applied

to me. These guys weren't "abusers."

In fact, one of them worked at a

local hospital on the Child Abuse

Prevention Committee.

No way did I want to see him lose

his job, because then he wouldn't

be able to give my mom

any more money.

"Children are helpless when it comes to someone hurting them. Don't cover up for anyone who violates our children."

"Make it clear to kids that they are in no way responsible or lacking just because a parent is an ass."

"Ladies: Never put a man before your kids."

Worthless
Male, age 32

Mom could afford to buy cocaine,

meth, and pot;

but helping me to pursue my goal

of becoming a professional musician

apparently was too expensive.

Or just not a priority. She said she'd

put me up for adoption if I ever told

anybody that she used drugs. She kept them

in the house; hid them in my room,

sometimes, thinking if the cops came in they

wouldn't search a kid's room.

Dad's frequent trips to the casinos took

precedence

over things like helping me buy a car,

and paying for school expenses.

My sister and I had to live with him whenever

mom was in jail.

He said it was a pain in the ass

to pay child support, and a pain in

the ass to raise kids.

When my parents divorced, neither one

of them wanted sole custody of us kids;

what does that tell you? Makes me wonder

why they even had kids

in the first place.

"No one has the right to make you feel worthless. Not even you."

"When I say that evil has to do with killing, I don't mean to restrict myself to corporeal murder. Evil is that which kills the spirit. There are various essential attributes of life-----particularly human life----such as sentience, mobility, awareness, growth, autonomy, will. It is possible to kill or attempt to kill one of those attributes without actually destroying the body. Thus, we may break a horse or even a child without harming a hair on his head."

(Dr. M. Scott Peck)

"Being a parent is being there through the tantrums, the milestones, and the tears. Being a parent means that you love that little person which you created more than you could ever love yourself or anybody else. You'd readily lose sleep to comfort them from their nightmares. You would risk your own life for that small person. Being a parent is never a burden; it's loving somebody else wholeheartedly and unconditionally for eternity. Being a parent is not a job. It is a privilege."

S.O.L.
Female, age 27

Statute of limitations.

I lost count of the times I have judged myself

because the asshole who abused me

didn't have to go to court for his crime.......

just because it took me years to get up

the courage to finally attempt to

press charges on him.

"You waited too long....." the District

Attorney said. I kept silent about the abuse

for most of my life; I was afraid

of retaliation.

Abuse kills-off a person just like

murder does; the SOL clock ticks,

but time doesn't heal.......it only hurts worse.

It takes away years that victims will never

get back.

SOL = Shit Outta Luck.

"Karma has no deadline."

Identity Theft
Male, age 42

Ralph. My parents called me Ralph

since I was born.

One day dad yelled at me

when I signed my name "Ralph"

on some registration papers

for kindergarten----told me I

was stupid,

Then he spelled what I was

supposed to write: R-O-G-E-R.

He said that was my "real" name;

the school didn't need to

know about R-A-L-P-H.

I didn't like the sound or feel of

R-O-G-E-R; it wasn't me.

Why did I have a "real" name

at school and a totally

different name at home?

Thirty-five years later,

still not ok with "Roger."

I went to court and changed my

name.

I changed it to Ralph.

"It shouldn't hurt to be a child."

"Sometimes you don't realize the weight of something you have been carrying until you feel the weight of its release."

Silent Night
Female, age 31

"You never said 'thank you' to me

 for those Christmas presents!"

my adoptive uncle shouted at me

on Christmas night.

"Santa brought them for me……" I responded.

I was confused. He told my sisters and I

That Santa Claus was coming

on Christmas Eve;

said that every year.

I tried to be good all year,

got good grades, did my chores;

sat on Santa's lap

at Macy's and told him

what I wanted for Christmas.

"Damn kids! Ungrateful!" my uncle

slammed the door and went to his car to

do a line of cocaine.

On his way out, he pushed the Christmas

tree over, and kicked the dog.

In therapy, when I was older, I found out

that my uncle had severe problems:

Narcissistic Personality Disorder.

It can't be cured.

That was the night my sisters and I

quit believing in Santa Claus.

It's hard to enjoy Christmas, anymore.

"There is no excuse for abuse, including the excuse of a personality disorder."

(Dr. Tara Palmatier)

Special
Male, age 34

My girlfriend was 32. I was 16.

She was my high school

English teacher.

I thought it was way cool

 that she took

an interest in <u>me</u>-----

out of the entire

high school she chose me.

She said I was special.

She made me promise

not to tell anyone about us.

I didn't tell anybody;

I loved her, and thought

she loved me.

It was my duty to protect

our relationship.

Later on I learned that it is

NEVER cool

to be in a relationship like that.

Certain kinds of secrets should NOT be kept.

I wish I'd told somebody.

"There is no greater agony than bearing an untold story inside you."

(Maya Angelou)

Something's Not Right
Female, age 37

I used to be a foster kid.

Before going into placement,

I thought

that all families were like mine;

physical fights between mom and dad,

one or the other in jail

for stupid things;

no appropriate boundaries, favoritism

amongst the kids,

everybody yelling

and arguing all the time.

Us kids weren't

supposed to talk about this at school.

In placement the kids were treated equally.

There was privacy and

 appropriate boundaries.

Cops weren't coming

over to break up fights between the parents,

or to arrest anybody.

Kids got allowance.

Growth was encouraged, not stifled.

At first, this all felt weird,

so very different from what

I was used to.

I think being in placement bought me

some time in the sense that I was

able to realize that there was something

not right with my family of origin. I didn't

know the words "abuse" or "Personality

Disorder"; but I could sense that

"something" wasn't quite right.

When I was returned to my

 family of origin,

I counted the years, months, and days

until I would turn 18

so as to get

out of there and

be on my own.

"Birds born in a cage think flying is an illness."

(Alejandro Jodorowski)

"You never know how strong you are until being strong is the only choice you have."

(Bob Marley)

Nobody Would Believe Me
Male Inmate, age 19

The psychologist tells my teachers

that I "make up wild stories."

Word got around amongst the faculty,

and nobody would take me seriously

from then on.

"That kid doesn't get enough attention

at home-----

he's just playing games,

telling tall tales at school,"

they'd say to each other

whenever my name came up.

Even if I had been playing games

that should've been an indication

that I needed help. Especially since all of

the "counseling" I was getting

apparently wasn't helping.

The psychologist covered his ass in advance.

Nobody would believe me if I ever

got up the nerve to report him for

sexual abuse. So I just stayed quiet about it.

Kept going to counseling with him

because if I didn't I would get sent to

the juvenile detention facility.

"If a child discloses abuse: Remain calm; believe the child; allow the child to talk; show

interest and concern; reassure and support the child; take action and report. This could save a child's life.
Don't: Panic or over-react; pressure the child to talk; promise anything you can't control; confront the offender; blame, or minimize the child's feelings; overwhelm the child with questions."

"Sociopaths never answer to facts. They always attack the messenger."

Vivid Imagination
Male, age 32

"I'll be filing for a divorce, soon," she said.

"You'll be 18 in two years----I'll be single

by then. We can get married."

Stringing me along with lies

to that effect.

She was 32, a staff person

at my group home;

She worked the night shift;

had sex with me in my

room when other kids were asleep.

I expected her to keep her promise.

Two years later,

I'm the bad guy for my expectations.

She told her husband and the cops

that I've been stalking her.

"That kid has a vivid imagination……

he thinks

I want to marry him."

Emotionally hanging by a thread,

suddenly abandoned.

Strung-out on anti-anxiety pills

to make the panic attacks go away.

"I used to think you took my breath away, but then I realized I was just suffocated by your bullshit."

Low Self-Esteem
Female, age 29

His body was found in a non-residential area.

Dead from a knife wound.

Homicide was ruled-out.

He was having affairs with vulnerable

young female

clients.

He used guilt-trip head games with them,

played on their low self-esteem,

so they wouldn't report him to his

licensing board.

One lady came forward, and her lawyer

was going to sue

for malpractice.

He stood to lose his psychotherapist

license…..and more. The story would hit

all of the news media.

He didn't care about his clients' mental health;

only about himself.

He never thought any of these clients

would say anything.

"Be careful who you trust and tell your problems to."

"It took me quite a long time to develop a voice and now that I have it I am not going to be silent."

Legally Guaranteed Silence
Female, age 41

A public school teacher sexually

abuses high school students;

he knows which kids

to select and groom: those from

messed-up families,

those who can keep secrets,

those who aren't loved at home and

look for love elsewhere.

He does this for many years....

never gets caught.

His victims are too scared to report him.

Except that one day a couple of victims

come forward;

one day, twelve years too late.

There is a civil compromise out of court;

very small money award for

all those years of abuse.

And there's a condition: these victims

have to continue

keeping this awful secret.

They have to heal from stolen

childhoods, low self-esteem, depression,

PTSD, and all that goes with it.

It is a struggle

to try to live a normal life……

for the rest of their lives.

In the meantime, the offender

remains employed at the school;

who knows how many more kids he

sexually abused……?

Years later he retires with full benefits.

He lives a normal life.

The school district never found out,

and perhaps never will; thanks to

the legal arrangement----if not a

guarantee---- of future silence

137

in his favor.

Something is definitely very wrong

with this picture.

"Please don't tell me what a great country we have until the children who get abused have more rights than the people who abuse them."

Dead Silence
Female, age 43

Professor Joe took advantage of many

college students for the duration

of his tenure.

There were the usual lies, broken promises,

and threats to students' lives.

He attacked their self-confidence, so they felt

undeserving of anyone better.

He killed his most recent "girlfriend."

When his prison time was nearly done,

 his ex-wife

and others pleaded with the Parole Board,

"Keep him locked up----

he's a danger

to society.

He totally disregards human life."

"Nearly 800,000 children younger than 18 are missing each year. That is an average of 2186 children reported missing every day."

Conclusion

Victims and survivors of abuse stay silent primarily for the following reasons:

1. They fear retaliation, punishment, death, harm to self/others/pets;

2. They feel a sense of obligation to protect the abuser because (s)he perceives the abuser as a source of "love";

3. They fear not being believed-----especially if the abuser is an esteemed professional member of the community.

The one thing in particular that I realized while writing this book is that it could not be written entirely in third-person informational "textbook" style. To present this document as a textbook lessens the emotional impact upon the reader ---- and, in effect, minimizes the victims' personal experiences. Therefore, I have taken statements of abuse victims with whom I have had the privilege of interviewing research purposes and para-phrased them. I am very grateful to the individuals who have allowed me to use their statements.

The accounts in this book are an extremely small representative sample of hundreds of thousands of incidents of abuse which occur on a daily basis throughout the world.

The following are the percentages of children who experienced maltreatment in the United States alone:

Neglect 62.8%

Physical abuse 16.6%

Sexual abuse 9.3%

Emotional/psychological abuse 7.1%

Medical neglect 2.0%

Other 14.3%

The 'Other' category listed above includes abandonment, threats to harm the child, congenital drug addiction and other situations that are not counted as specific individual categories in these particular statistics. The percentages here add up to more than 100 percent because some children were victims of more than one type of maltreatment

(USDHHShttp://www.acf.hhs.gov/programs/cb; NCANDS http://www.ndacan.cornell.edu)

Everyone who has experienced child abuse in any form deserves to be heard. Every victim and survivor should be empowered, encouraged to speak out, and believed.
Hopefully, someday the legal system will change existing practices so that the silencing tactics by abusers and enablers will stop or, better yet, not even have a chance to begin.

I would like to see more programs implemented in our schools which focus on teaching kids of all ages how to recognize abusive conduct by adults and, most importantly, never to keep quiet about inappropriate and abusive adult conduct.

With regard to children of Narcissistic parents who experience emotional abuse on a daily basis, the best that can be done, since Narcissistic Personality Disorder is not curable, is to strengthen the children's self-esteem via counseling and educational programs which would be designed for this. If children can't get appropriate nurturing at home, then they need to have it provided for them elsewhere. Otherwise, many will LOOK for it elsewhere in surrogate street "families" such as gangs and organized crime.

Mindset

Serial killers. Serial sex abusers.

Same mindset. Same effects.

Both of these:

Have specific victims whom they target;

Plan their crimes-----these are not accidents;

Have specific modus operandi;

Totally disregard their victims;

Try to hide evidence of their crimes;

Silence their victims;

Repeat their crimes;

Are incurable and cannot be rehabilitated.

In both types of crimes the victims' lives are lost

and their time is stolen.

There is no statute of limitations for murder;

so there shouldn't

be one for sexual abuse crimes.

(Terri Austin, Ph.D, J.D.)

RECOMMENDED READING

Austin, Terri (2006). *Unfair Advantage: Sexual Abuse by Psychotherapists, Priests, and Police.* Trafford Publishing, Canada

Barnes, Wendy (2015). *And Life Continues: Sex Trafficking and My Journey to Freedom.* CreateSpace Independent Publishing Platform

Bass, Ellen (1991). *I Never Told Anyone: Writings by Women Survivors of Child Sexual Abuse.* Harper Collins Publishers. NY

Brett, Drew (2014). *Narcissist As Parent.* Drew Brett Publications

Clemens, Andrea (2015). *Invisible Target: Breaking the Cycle of Educator Sexual Abuse.* Hickory Nut Publishers

Hobson, Charles (2012). *Passing the Trash: A Parent's Guide to Combat Sexual Abuse/Harassment of Their Children in School.* CreateSpace Independent Publishing Platform

Merryn, Erin (2013). *An Unimaginable Act: Overcoming and Preventing Child Abuse Through Erin's Law.* Health Communications, Inc. Deerfield Beach, Florida.

Payson, Eleanor (2002). *Wizard of Oz and Other Narcissists: Coping with the One-Way Relationship in Work, Love, and Family.* Julian Day Publishing, MI

Tom, C. (2014). *Pedophile Priest .* CreateSpace Independent Publishing Platform

Van Dam, Carla (2001). *Identifying Child Molesters: Preventing Child Sexual Abuse by Recognizing the Patterns of the Offenders*, 1st Edition. Routledge Publishing

ONLINE RESOURCES

Advocate Web
http://www.advocateweb.org

Bishop Accountability
http://www.bishop-accountability.org

California Rescue Dogs Association
http://search-dogs.carda.org

Child Matters: Educating to Prevent Child Abuse
http://www.childmatters.org.nz/86/learn-about-child-abuse/recognise-the-signs/emotional-abuse

Child Molestation Research and Prevention Institute
http://www.childmolestationprevention.org/pages/tell_others_the_facts.html

Child Welfare Information Gateway
https://www.childwelfare.gov/topics/systemwide/laws-policies/statutes/report

CopWatch: Policing the Police
http://www.copwatch.com

Federal Bureau of Investigation
https://www.fbi.gov/wanted

Internet Crime Complaint Center
http://www.ic3.gov/media/2015/150611.aspx

Light's House: Escaping from Stockholm
http://www.lightshouse.org/escaping-from-stockholm.html#axzz2GB7CmCgd

Marc Klaas Foundation
http://klaaskids.org

Megan's Law: Sex Offender Locator
http://www.meganslaw.com

Narcissism 101
http://www.narcissism101.com/index.html

Narcissism Free: Recovering from Narcissistic Abuse
http://www.narcissismfree.com

Ntnl Association to Protect Children
http://www.protect.org

Ntnl Center for Missing and Exploited Children
http://www.missingkids.com/home

Police Abuse
http://www.policeabuse.com

Rape, Abuse, Incest, National Network
http://apps.rainn.org/policy-crime-definitions/index.cfm?state=Californiaandgroup=7

Safe At Home: Domestic Violence, Stalking, Abuse
http://www.sos.ca.gov/registries/safe-home

Scouts Child Abuse Prevention
http://www.ppbsa.org/volunteer/child_abuse_prevention/index.htm

Search and Rescue Dogs of the United States
http://www.sardogsus.org

Sex Offender Search
http://offenders.sexoffenderrecord.com/sex-offender-search

Sex Offender Updates
http://sexoffenderupdates.com

Silent Edge: Sexual Abuse in Sports
http://www.silent-edge.org

SOL Reform
http://sol-reform.com

Stop Educator Sexual Abuse
http://www.sesamenet.org

Survivors Network of those Abused by Priests
http://www.snapnetwork.org

Therapy Exploitation Link Line
http://www.therapyabuse.org

Together We Heal
http://together-we-heal.org

Verbal Abuse Journals
http://verbalabusejournals.com/about-abuse/brainwashing-and-domestic-abuse/brainwashing-steps/#.UPXgcofB9SI.facebook

References

American Psychiatric Association (2013). *Diagnostic and Statistical Manual of Mental Disorders, Fifth Edition.* Washington, D.C.

Moylan, Carrie A., Herrenkohl, T., Sousa, C., et al. (2010). *The Effectsof Child Abuse and Exposure to Domestic Violence on Adolescent Internalizing and Externalizing Behavior Problems.* Journal of Family Violence. January; 25(1): 53–63.

http://www.ncbi.nlm.nih.gov/pmc/articles/PMC2872 483/

NCANDS (http://www.ndacan.cornell.edu)

Tuthill, Oliver (1998). *Understanding the Six Forms of Emotional Abuse.* Autumn Tree Productions, http://www.worldcat.org/title/understanding-the-six-forms-of-emotional-child-abuse/oclc/43980174

USDHHS http://www.acf.hhs.gov/programs/cb